THREE Early American Folk Hymns for Piano

arranged by Rodney Abriol

Table of Contents

My Shepherd Will Supply My Need

Rodney Abriol
based on the tune RESIGNATION
from *Southern Harmony*, 1835

Simply and unhurried ♩ = ca. 66

25
Ped.
Ped.
simile
29
p
33
Dolce
Ped.
Ped.
simile
36
39
mp

mf
pedal harmonically
8va
rit.
p

57
a tempo
Ped.
simile
60
63
With confidence
f
66
8va
69

72
più f
75
8va
78
mf
81
pedal harmonically
84

87
8va
rit.
p
a tempo
espress.
Ped.
90
Ped.
simile
93
rit.
a tempo
Ped.
96
dim.
Ped.
99
pp
rit.
8va
Ped.

There's a Land That Is Fairer Than Day

Rodney Abriol
based on the tune SWEET BY AND BY
by Joseph Philbrick Webster, 1868

F0674

11
mp
Ped.
14
simile
mf
17
espress.
mp
pedal harmonically
20
Ped.
simile
22
mp

24
27
30
mf
Ped.
Ped.
Ped.
33
simile
f
36
espress.
mp
pedal harmonically

39
mf
simile
42
f
45
espress.
mf
rit.
Slower
mp
pedal harmonically
48
Tempo I ♩= 80
p
simile
51
pp
rit.

Oh, When Shall I See Jesus

Rodney Abriol
based on the tune THE MORNING TRUMPET
from *The Sacred Harp*, 1844

Steady and smooth ♩= 108

F0674

20
24
p
8vb
28
Ped.
Ped.
Ped.
Ped.
simile
32
Ped.
Ped.
36
Ped.
Ped.
Ped.
Ped.
simile

40
mp
Ped.
44
Ped.
simile
48
52
mf
56
rit.

a tempo
simile
accel.
mp
Fast and light ♩= 112
mf
simile
p

75
78
Resolutely ♩= 132
f
8vb
81
più f
84
Tempo I
(♩= 108)
mp
87
p

91
95
Fast and light ♩= 112
accel.
mp
simile
8vb
98
100
mf
102
simile
mp

105
107
mf
110
f
Broad and strong ♩= 66
113
8vb
Ped.
116
ff